W9-BNE-433

Should I Keep My Baby?

Martha Zimmerman

BETHANY HOUSE PUBLISHERS

MINNEAPOLIS, MINNESOTA 55438

A Division of Bethany Fellowship, Inc.

Scripture quotations, unless otherwise indicated, are from the New American Standard Bible.

Copyright © 1983
Martha Zimmerman
All Rights Reserved

Published by Bethany House Publishers
A Division of Bethany Fellowship, Inc.
6820 Auto Club Road, Minneapolis, Minnesota 55438

Printed in the United States of America

Library of Congress Cataloging in Publication Data

Zimmerman, Martha, 1934-
  Should I keep my baby.

  1. Young women—Sexual behavior. 2. Pregnant
women. 3. Mother and child. 4. Young women—
Religious life. 5. Abortion. I. Title.
HQ27.5.Z55   1983   362.1'982'0088055   83-6068
ISBN 0-87123-578-1 (pbk.)

Should I Keep My Baby?

This book is dedicated
to *you*

IF YOU THINK YOU MIGHT BE PREGNANT

If you have
> had sexual intercourse (even if only once)
> missed a menstrual period
> feelings of nausea, either when you wake up
> > or later in the day
> tender or enlarged breasts
> frequent urination
> unusual mood changes . . .

it's important that you go *immediately* for a pregnancy test. Don't put it off one more day. It really will be better in every way to know for sure.

The test itself is a simple procedure. Either a blood or urine sample will be analyzed, and you will know the results by the next day. A number of places offer this service, such as your local

> Department of Health
> Hospital
> Health Center
> Birthright Organization
> Crisis Pregnancy Center (see page 88)
> Private Doctor
> National Adoption Hotline (202/463-7563)

Open your telephone directory. Call one of these agencies. Ask about fees. The cost generally varies from *free* to about $20. Make an appointment!

Kits for pregnancy testing are sold at most drugstores. If you choose this method, follow the directions *very* carefully. If the results are positive, you will need to confirm them with a doctor. If the test results are negative, it is possible that you still might be pregnant. Continue to pay attention to the signals your body is sending.

PREFACE

You are pregnant. It may seem unreal. But now you know it's true.

Your story and the circumstances surrounding this event in your life are uniquely yours. Somehow this has happened to you. The tests were positive. Your body has been "hinting," and now all of your "wondering" has been confirmed.

DON'T PANIC!

What you do now, how you approach what has happened, is *very important*. Some crucial decisions will have to be made. It's so much better to think through all of the possibilities and all the consequences of your choices than to react hastily to your situation.

I expect there are all kinds of emotions running around inside of you—with many questions repeatedly popping up:

How can this be happening to me?

What will my boyfriend say?

What will my parents say?

What will my friends think of me?

What should I do *now*?

Before we go any further, I want you to know that I care, even though I do not know you personally. I want to help. But much more important than my support is this promise: *God cares.* He really does! He loves you, pregnant and all! I keep two Bible-verse plaques on my desk to remind me of His love. They are special messages that say, "God demonstrates His own love toward us, in that while we were yet sinners, Christ died for us" (Rom. 5:8) and ". . . I will not forget you. Behold, I have inscribed you on the palms of My hands" (Isa. 49:15-16).

You don't have to "do" anything in order to gain God's attention. The One who made you watches and cares. His love is unconditional. He is waiting for you to get in touch with Him, to unload "all your anxiety upon Him, because He cares for you" (1 Pet. 5:7).

So far, I have talked about you and God. What about your family? Your friends? Your baby's father? And, most importantly, your baby? I will guide you in asking yourself some questions that will eventually lead to: "What is best for *everyone* in light of the circumstances?" At this point in your life, I'm sure that seems overwhelming. So we'll take it a step at a time. It is important that you try hard to see the whole picture.

You are probably getting an avalanche of advice from some of the people mentioned above—if anyone else knows you're pregnant (if not, I'll give you some suggestions on how to tell them). Assume they mean well. You need all the support you can get. But not all of the counsel will be helpful. Remember, it is hard for these people to give unbiased advice. Some are inclined to make recommendations based on how your decision will affect them. Pressures have a way of building. So take this book and slip away to a favorite place where you can be alone. Get comfortable, and let me present some questions you should answer and some alternatives you should consider. *Please* weigh them carefully. I want to help you arrive at conclusions that are yours, that are right for *you,* and that you won't regret later. Since you must live with yourself, I want you to *like* yourself and be pleased with your decisions, way down inside.

Throughout this book you will read real stories about real people. Names and some details have been changed to protect their privacy, but the facts are accurate. Many girls have shared themselves—their thoughts, experiences, feelings, solutions and prayers—to help you. I'm sure you will join me in thanking them. My deep appreciation goes to Carol Johnson, my editor, for her challenge and prayerful support; to Joanne Fankhauser and Betty Phillips, my typists; and to Steve Hayner, University Pastor, University Presbyterian Church, Seattle, for the Bible study questions in Chapter 5, written especially for this book.

Martha Zimmerman
Richland, Washington

CONTENTS

Imagine. . .

You are holding a big bouquet of roses.
It isn't a nice, trim arrangement prepared by
    a florist.
Instead, it's bulky and awkward—
Almost too big to handle.
The thorns prick you and they hurt.
No vase seems large enough to hold
    all the flowers.
No clever shape seems to contain them
    completely.
Forcing the stems might break them.
But you want to keep all the flowers fresh
    and beautiful.
At least you want to try.

You have some choices.

The people and problems in your life are like this
    bouquet.
The problems seem huge.
The people sometimes seem unbending.
Many will be affected by your decisions.
You sincerely want the best solution
    to your present situation.

You *do* have some choices.

1

YOU ARE HOLDING THE BOUQUET

"What Should I Do?"

You probably didn't think this would happen to you. But it did. In the beginning it's hard to believe—even to understand. You probably don't *feel* anything yet. You certainly don't *look* any different; nothing shows. But you have been told, "The test is positive. You are going to have a baby."

The news that you are pregnant may have turned you into an emotional popcorn popper. With stunned disbelief you may feel worried, angry, guilty, excited, stupid, bitter, scared, dazed, up-tight, trapped, nervous, resentful, used, ashamed, alone, depressed, caught and overwhelmed. I'm sure you never thought *you* would be the one to get pregnant.

Now it's time to think hard, plan carefully, and act wisely. You need to look at the options, weigh the consequences and compare the results of the various choices. But as I promised, we will take it a step at a time.

Before you read another paragraph, promise me you won't close this book or lay it aside unfinished.

Please read it clear through with an open heart and mind. I won't be trying to force you into a certain decision. I simply want to help you come to the conclusion that is right for *you*. Therefore, we're going to consider together the options before you. (*Consider* means to think about with care and caution.)

First, let's consider briefly the physical events that are taking place in your body. A tiny, naked embryo has stopped your periods. In order to make your womb "livable," a protective capsule of fluid has developed around this growing embryo. Within three weeks after conception, this embryo—your baby—has a beating heart, a brain, and the beginnings of limbs. (At that time you probably didn't even know you were pregnant.) If you have passed the fourth week, your baby has developed the first traces of eyes, ears and nose, and all its organs. By now you have missed a period (or maybe you are still hoping you are just late).

By the second month, the heart has begun to beat regularly and circulation has started. The brain is functioning and brain waves can be detected. Scarcely an inch long, the embryo looks like a tiny person with a definite little face. In the third month—8 to 12 weeks—elbows and knees, fingers and toes, including soft nails, become recognizable. At this point, 95 percent of the baby's structure and organs are complete.

Contained in your womb is a nameless, voiceless, developing human being. This tiny individual can be tested, treated, examined and x-rayed; the baby can receive transfusions and undergo surgery—or he can be destroyed by abortion.

Abortion is an option considered by many girls as they face an unexpected, unwanted pregnancy. According to the current laws, every pregnant woman has the right to "terminate her pregnancy," during the first six months* if for some reason she does not want to have a baby. People have written many pamphlets and articles on the subject of abortion. Often they emphasize the absolute right of the baby or the absolute right of the mother. This is inappropriate, as both must be considered. Because abortions are legal, they have become a popular method of "disposing of a problem." Many call it "freedom of choice." "Choice" suggests that more than one course of action is open to you. "Freedom" means that legally no one can force you to carry this pregnancy to full term. It also means that no one can force you to snuff out the life of your child. You not only are allowed to choose, you *have* to choose.

But just because it's "legal" to have an abortion doesn't mean it's best or morally right to have one. A popular notion often discussed today has to do with *your rights.* Stop just a minute; I'm going to be hard on you—briefly. You do have the right to control your own body, and you should. You have a right to choose how far your sexual relationships should go. But once you have had intercourse and pregnancy occurs, then, even though the newly conceived human life is *in* your body and dependent *upon* your body, it's *not* your body. Therefore, to say that the

*Since there is no medical procedure which can determine exactly how far along a pregnancy is, some abortions are being performed much later than six months.

embryo is "part of my body and at my disposal" is not really fair or true. Now that conception has taken place, *another* genetically unique life is inside you. Your baby's rights must be considered right alongside yours.

The value of the developing infant in you does not depend on its being "wanted." Just because *you* may not want the baby cannot be taken as an excuse for abortion. Dan is a good example. He was born in a filling station restroom, then abandoned in a trash can. He certainly wasn't "wanted." Dan, telling his story, said, "Thank God someone came and found me, or I could have been dead!" He is now a happy, fulfilled adult.

There are thousands of couples in this country who *want* very badly to have a child, but are unable to conceive their own. Therefore, an abortion performed on the pretext of saving the child from being "unwanted" is not even logical. Assuredly , someone *does* want your baby. Think about it.

Most of us would rather not think or read about how abortions are performed. However, in order to help you make an informed decision, you need to understand what takes place in an abortion. The following section describes what would happen if you had your baby aborted.

There are five major techniques for abortion. A common method for ending a pregnancy before the twelfth or thirteenth week is called the *D & C*, which stands for *dilation and curettage*. In this procedure, the surgeon stretches your cervix (dilation) and inserts a tiny, hoelike instrument into your uterus through the vagina. The surgeon then scrapes the wall of the uterus (curettage), cutting the baby's body to pieces, and scraping the placenta away from the wall of the uterus. There is considerable bleeding. Forcing, or manually opening the cervix weakens this muscle. In a later pregnancy, carrying a baby to term may be more difficult because this important muscle has been weakened.

A second method for ending an early pregnancy, which is often simpler as well as safer, is called *suction abortion*. For this, the surgeon dilates your cervix and inserts a powerful suction tube into the uterus. Working like a vacuum cleaner, it tears to pieces the developing baby and placenta, and sucks them into a jar. The destroyed parts of the baby are recognizable. If you are further along in your pregnancy, these two methods are too dangerous because they can cause heavy bleeding.

The third abortion technique, used after sixteen weeks, is called the *saline abortion*, or "salting out." By this stage in the pregnancy, enough amniotic fluid has collected in the sac around the baby for a long needle to be inserted through your abdomen directly into this sac. A solution of concentrated salt is then injected into the amniotic fluid. The salt solution invades and destroys the baby's lungs and digestive tract. At the same time the baby's outer layer of skin is burned off. It usually takes about an hour to end the life of the baby with this method. You, the mother, would go into labor about a day later and your baby would be delivered dead.

The fourth procedure is called a *hysterotomy*. This technique is exactly the same as a caesarean section, with one major difference: a hysterotomy is performed to *end* the baby's life; a caesarean section is usually performed to *save* the baby's life. A hysterotomy is used after the fourteenth week. In this procedure your abdomen is surgically opened, as is the uterus. The baby is lifted out, along with the placenta, and discarded.

Babies aborted by this method are, of course, small; but they have been know to move their little arms and legs, breathe, and try to cry. Hysterotomy babies are born alive but are left to die.

The newest method is the *prostaglandin chemical abortion*. This hormone-like compound, either applied or injected into the uterus, causes this muscle to contract. This is actually premature labor. The intense contractions push out the baby. Many babies aborted this way also have been born alive.

Extreme viewpoints, vicious arguments, and strong emotions characterize the abortion issue. Legal, medical, psychological, and religious experts all have different opinions.

In spite of the current debates , the biologists who have studied human life at all stages agree that life begins when the sperm and egg unite at conception. Therefore, the embryo, at whatever state of development, is *wholly* human and deserves to be valued and treated as such. Because of this, abortion at any stage is an extremely serious matter.

The single cell, the combination of the egg which your body produced and the sperm from your boyfriend, is, though tiny, a complete human being—unless some force destroys its life. After conception, nothing new will be added until its death as an adult person. What occurs between conception and death is simply growth and development. Destroying it at any point is, biologically, taking a human life.

To deny that the unborn is a person at any stage of development involves a great amount of rationalizing and presumption. Authorities from many fields don't agree as to the beginning of "personhood." One *reliable* authority, however, is the Bible—God's word to us. It contains important insights into this problem.

The Bible often mentions children, both unborn and born, and it never refers to them in any way other than as full-fledged people. Psalm 139:13-16 describes God's personal involvement in David's *unborn* life: "For Thou didst form my inward parts; Thou didst weave me in my mother's womb. . . . My frame was not hidden from Thee, when I was made in secret. . . ." If David had been the only person to write this thought, we might say he was just being poetic. But other Bible writers said the same thing. The prophet Isaiah wrote, "The Lord called me from the womb" (49:1); God said to Jeremiah, "Before I formed you in the womb I knew you, and before you were born I consecrated you" (1:5); and the Apostle Paul, hundreds of years later, wrote, "He who had set me apart, even from my mother's womb. . ." (Gal.

1:15). The beginning or meaning of "personhood" did not seem complicated to these men.

These Bible verses, when added to the understanding of the biologists, lead to the conclusion that the unborn baby *is* a person.

If you are considering an abortion as the answer to your problem, remember that you cannot rely on what's "legal" to justify your actions; authorities keep changing their minds and the laws, so today's right could be tomorrow's wrong. Your decision would be easier if there were a simple way of drawing a line so that abortion before a certain stage of pregnancy would be *morally* right. Since conception means a developing baby exists, the line has been drawn. Life began at conception and leaves no room for an abortion "of convenience." Laws cannot change this fact. What is *legal* is not necessarily *moral.*

I don't know your circumstances, but *you* do. So rather than my telling you what to do, please answer the following questions. Then you can come to your own decision about abortion.

1. *How responsible am I for being pregnant?*
2. *To what extent is my pregnancy the result of my own choices? (Contraceptives can fail or be used carelessly; you cannot "blame" your pregnancy on a faulty contraceptive. "No" is the only foolproof contraceptive.)*
3. *Did I deliberately try to get pregnant?*
4. *Before I became pregnant, did I believe that abortion was wrong and that I would never have one?*

5. *Or, did I think there was nothing wrong with abortion?*

Whatever your views were previously, your pregnancy will cause you to test your feelings and ideas about abortion. Do not allow the pressures of the moment to force you into a decision you may regret all your life.

Here is another valid question to ask yourself: *Is the baby which is growing in my body competing for my life?* If it appears you can't physically live through this pregnancy and will die if you go to full term, then you should *consider* an abortion. Certain medical risks exist with pregnancy, but advances in medical technology make this concern very minimal. Pregnancy rarely threatens a woman's life. Your doctor will tell you if your life is actually in danger. Ask him, then ask God to help you decide. God's grace means that we have the assurance of His forgiveness and help when we are up against choices of this kind.

Is your *mental* health being threatened? This question pits the life of your baby against your own personal wholeness. Look at this argument carefully. The first thoughts that came to your mind might have been: *Pregnant? It's not fair! I got caught! No way am I going to go through the embarrassment and nuisance of being pregnant with a baby I don't want. I can't handle it! I'll be a wreck!*

Here I must caution you that carrying, for the rest of your life, the guilt from having had an abortion can also threaten your emotional and mental health.

A girl who has had an abortion carries a heavy psychological burden. A pastor with over twenty years' counseling experience says, "Every time a woman begins to tell me about her abortion, she cries, regardless of her age or when the abortion took place—whether it was years ago or just recently." I have had the same experience when talking with young women.

A psychiatrist-obstetrician who has performed abortions says, "I think every woman—whatever her age, her background, or sexuality—has a trauma ending a pregnancy. A psychological price is paid...." An abortion is a destructive act, not only toward the baby but also toward yourself.

If you still lean toward having an abortion, *make a list of your reasons.* You must not decide to end the life of the baby on a whim just because being pregnant is embarrassing or inconvenient. Abortion should never be thought of as an automatic choice or used as an easy way out. Realize you can't exclude your feelings, but be prepared to back up your decision with a list of good logical reasons—*why* you are thinking about terminating your pregnancy. Even if you have favored abortion in the past, take time to reconsider as you test your feelings about *this* abortion. Your personal involvement may change the way you think and feel about this matter. If the desire to keep your sex life and pregnancy a "secret" is pushing you toward an abortion, please think carefully about your decision. Remember, another human life is at stake.

Don't sneak off to an abortion service that is less

than adequate, in an attempt to hide the event and thus endanger your life. And don't ask someone else, such as a counselor, to make this decision for you. If you have an abortion, but later feel it was the wrong choice, you will try to blame the person who made the decision. This short-circuits your responsibility and will hinder your emotional maturity and growth.

If you are opposed to abortion, *make a list of your reasons.* Again, use logic but don't ignore your feelings.

Let me tell you how Mary came to her decision. She says: "From the beginning I knew I couldn't have an abortion. I already knew how I felt about the issue before I was the one who was pregnant. I wouldn't have been honest with myself if I had changed my position just because it was happening to me."

Why are you going to carry your baby to birth? Is it because you believe an abortion destroys a human life? Or are you afraid to have an abortion?

Of course, pregnancy involves a certain degree of risk. However, an abortion involves a great deal of risk—physical, mental, and emotional. Some doctors think that pregnancy in young girls may impair their health. But other doctors believe that abortions in young girls may impair their health *and* their ability to have children later in life. Statistics can support either side of the issue. You have a lot to think about with much at stake! Remember, being pregnant is *natural.* An abortion is *unnatural.* It interrupts the normal process of life.

I'm sure you have guessed my goal is to carefully

caution you against abortion. Abortion is *not* a solution to a social problem or personal embarrassment. To try to "cover up" an "accident" will only complicate your life. If you think you must abort your baby to keep your boyfriend, think a minute; the fact is that an abortion tends to drive a couple *apart* rather than draw them together. And abortion, quite simply, is the destruction of an unborn baby who is perceived to be a problem. Only you can decide what to do. I urge you, make your decision very carefully.

If you decide to have an abortion, you will need spiritual and emotional help when it is over. One of the greatest gifts God offers us is the help of other people. Every girl who has shared her story mentions the need for supportive people. You should find someone to whom you can talk.

If you decide to have the baby, accept that responsibility and get good medical care as early in the pregnancy as possible—RIGHT NOW! You will improve the chances that you will both be healthy when you give birth.

So, let's assume, for now, that you are going to keep your baby—at least until you finish reading this book. The dictionary defines *pregnant* as: "being with young; full of importance; full of significance." It no longer matters *how* or *why* you got pregnant. The fact is *you are pregnant.* Inside of you is a baby, a tiny person, preparing for birth. Ahead of you is a very important task, which is to nurture and protect the growing baby.

Your decision will have eternal significance. And what you believe will influence what you decide. It's not easy to do what is unpleasant for the sake of what you believe; but what you do now will become your personal statement about the value of human life.

2

THE FLOWERS IN YOUR BOUQUET

"Whom Should I Tell?"

"Admit your faults to one another and pray for each other so that you may be healed" (James 5:16a, TLB).

It may seem like no one could possibly understand your pregnancy. You may wish you could keep it a secret. It isn't easy to admit: "I have a problem."

Your whole world is changing! It's hard to think straight. You may not want to think at all. It would be easier to withdraw, stay in bed with the covers pulled over your head, sleep all the time, cry a lot, become a TV addict, or sit around feeling sorry for yourself. You may try shifting your feelings into neutral . . . numbness sets in . . . you can't feel the pain—but something *always* jars you awake or jabs you with memories. Pretending, wishing, hoping, or ignoring won't make the problem go away. But you're sure you'll go crazy if you don't tell someone.

You have probably asked yourself:

"Whom should I tell?"

"How should I tell my family?"

"What will people say?"

"What will they think?"

"What will happen to my relationship with..." (take a minute and name the important people in your life).

"Where will I live until the baby is born?"

"Who will listen to me? Who will understand my feelings?"

"How can *anyone* help?"

"What am I going to do?"

"Whom Should I Tell?"

Mom? Dad? An older sister? Your boyfriend? An aunt? A teacher? A Young Life leader or Campus Life director? Your church's youth director? A girlfriend's mother? Your pastor, priest or rabbi? A school counselor? A friend? Choose carefully. Find someone you respect, someone you can trust; one who can keep a secret; who is sensible, wise and kind; who is a good listener; someone who will *care*. (You may have already told someone, and possibly that person gave you this book.)

You need understanding and love (love includes forgiveness); but your own strong feelings of independence are also good. Too many people try to dump their problems in someone else's lap, place the blame on someone else's shoulders, or expect someone else to solve everything. Maintain a sensible "balance." Try hard to accept personal responsibility for your actions and decisions.

But no one expects you to bear this by yourself. You need not go through it alone. Choose someone to help and then talk with her/him. You need support. Your family may be the best ones to turn to for help.

"How Should I Tell My Family?"

What is your relationship with your family? Do you have strong ties with them? Or "average" ties that might be strained or collapse under the stress of your pregnancy? Or weak ties with a history of misunderstandings, poor communication and broken relationships?

It would be best to tell your family right away. Trying to keep this a secret from your parents may force you to lie or create a sneaky cover-up.

You may be thinking:

"But I'm afraid to tell my folks. It will just kill them," or "They don't care about me. It won't make any difference," or something in between.

The news of your pregnancy will probably hurt your parents, but it is not likely to kill them. More than likely they will find out sometime. And, speaking as a parent, I would rather know, and know *now*, than to find out later—possibly from someone else. Your parents should hear it from *you*. After the shock waves have passed you may be surprised at the deeper relationship that has developed. When a major problem arises, people often draw closer together for strength.

In the Chinese language, the symbols for *danger* and *opportunity* are combined to form the word *crisis*. You are in a crisis. If the thought of telling your parents frightens you, consider several possible ways to go about it. If you can't just "tell" them, try writing a letter. Mail it, or put it where they will be sure to find it or, best of all, give it to them personally. Then ask them to sit down and talk with you. Allow plenty of time to work it through. Plan your approach. You know your parents, their way of dealing with problems, their habits *and* the "right" time to speak with them. If you aren't living at home, you might call them on the telephone.

Susan knew she had to tell her mother. Her approach was straightforward and simple: "I think I'm pregnant, Mom. I've missed a period." Together they went for her pregnancy test, and it was positive. But now Susan had an ally, her mother, who helped by telling her husband the news. She also told him, "Susan's pretty upset. It won't help matters if you yell at her." So he didn't.

Diane handled telling her parents another way. She had left home and was living with foster parents when she got pregnant. Afraid that her parents might become violent and physically harm her, she arranged to have a neutral person, her social worker, present. They were invited to one of the worker's counseling sessions where Diane told them. Eventually Diane was able to move back home. Her parents were supportive during the rest of her pregnancy.

If you are having difficulty with your family, you might feel more comfortable telling the news in the presence of your pastor, priest or rabbi; your teacher; or a third party whom they respect. Regardless of how bad the relationship with your parents has been, include them in your current crisis.

I've written a letter to your parents and included it at the back of this book (see p. 95). If you think it might help, feel free to cut it out or make a copy and give it to them.

What you do next will depend upon your situation and your family's response to your pregnancy. Don't jump to any conclusions before they have had time to hear you, talk about it, think, pray and respond.

You may need help in solving some of the following problems:

"Where Will I Live Until the Baby Is Born?"

You may be able to live at home. You may need to move across the state. Trusted friends or relatives are often willing to help. In some cities, you can arrange to live in a private home with a caring family who will accept and treat you as a member of their family. Depending on your circumstances, your financial situation and specific needs, this may be a good option. Some large cities also have group homes or maternity residences where up to several pregnant girls live together.

Another consideration is your schooling. If you are still in high school, I strongly urge you to stay in school as long as possible. Most schools are very cooperative in arranging schedules, private tutoring or whatever you might need. Do whatever you can to continue your schooling. Check with your guidance counselor or principal.

Several agencies are prepared to help you decide where to live: various church-sponsored organizations (Adventists, Catholic Family Services, Lutheran Social Services, etc.), Birthright, The Salvation Army, to name a few. I also recommend you contact one or more of the following organizations: Evangelical Child and Family Agency (312/653-6400); Bethany Christian Services (616/459-6273); your nearest Crisis Pregnancy Center (see p. 88); National Committee for Adoption (202/463-7563). These organizations have offices across the country. You need not belong to any of these churches or agencies for them to help you. Call and find out what's available.

"Who Will Listen to Me? Who Will Understand My Feelings?"

This will depend on who you are and what your specific situation is like. Close friends (or a family member who is also a close friend) often make good listeners. Certain friends will listen and then tell you what you *want* to hear. Other friends will listen and then tell you what you *need* to hear. Both kinds of friends will be helpful as you seek direction and guidance. If your friends know about your pregnancy and don't mention it, or even seem to ignore or avoid you, don't interpret their actions as not caring about you. They may care very much but just don't know how to express their concern. That's why you might want to find a special kind of friend, a professional counselor who is not emotionally involved in your life. Such a person is often very helpful and is prepared to provide valuable information and support.

In an effort to meet your social, spiritual, and emotional needs, a professionally qualified, experienced counselor will listen in a nonjudgmental way and help you work through your social, spiritual, and emotional problems. Look for someone with a good reputation for reliable counseling.

You will face decisions in such matters as: marriage, education, housing, medical services, financial assistance, adoptive-placement counseling, self-forgiveness and self-acceptance.

In the midst of the many decisions you must make, a trained counselor will listen and then help you sort out your relationships and responsibilities. In an atmosphere of acceptance and understanding, he/she will allow you to express your feelings and will assist you in regaining your self-esteem. A counselor can guide you by suggesting educational options, or vocational training and job opportunities—not a way *out* but a way *through*. Your counselor also will help with adjustments following the delivery of your baby so that you can live a full, satisfying life.

Sally went to Catholic Family Services for help. There she met with a counselor once a week and received wonderful support. She was encouraged to talk about her future and make specific plans for after the baby was born.

Contrary to popular opinion, *many* adults care! Pastors, doctors, lawyers, teachers and the agencies I've suggested can put you in touch with agency counselors who will help you cope with your situation, and deal with family-related problems as well as your emotional conflicts.

You are not alone! God offers you a marvelous gift of help: other people. Crisis lines and telephone-counseling ministries are available twenty-four hours a day if you need to talk to someone. I have heard girls say, "Taking the first step, making the first call, is the hardest." You don't have to identify yourself, though later you may want to. If the first person can't help, please don't give up. Try again. Call and ask questions until you get the answers you need. There really are people out there who care about you. I promise!

3

A THORN AMONG ROSES

Before Saying, "I Do"

It's a fact! Roses have thorns. Most people, even when careful, get pricked when they hold these flowers. In spite of the hazards, they are drawn to their beauty. Life has its roses—and thorns. Love does, too. You are a beautiful young woman, full of potential. But it would be naive of me to think there is no pain in your life, no thorn.

So what can you do about the thorn problem? The Apostle Paul *lived* the answer. He encountered huge problems throughout his life. Then, to top it off, there was given to him what he called "a thorn in the flesh" (2 Cor. 12:7). Ouch! Only God knows what the "thorn" actually was. But more important than knowing Paul's specific problem is understanding the solution God gave Paul: "My grace is sufficient for you, for power is perfected in weakness" (2 Cor. 12:9). God is able and willing to help you through the hurts!

So, whose fault is it that you are pregnant? I would guess you have asked yourself, "What went wrong?" Yes, I know you didn't get pregnant alone! What about him? You may have believed that you were "in love" when you and your boyfriend had sex together. On the other hand, you may have been conned or manipulated into it. The reasons, whatever they were, are not really the issue now. The important fact to look at squarely and accept is that you are responsible for the decision you made (yes, it was a decision even though it may not have seemed like one at the time), and you are responsible for the decision you make now.

There was a time when "shotgun weddings" were the common solution, if an unmarried girl got pregnant. Her father forced the boy who "did it" to marry his daughter. People often joked and made fun of this serious situation; but, in fact, the Bible places a heavy responsibility on a father to determine what is best for his unmarried, pregnant daughter (see Ex. 22:16-17; Num. 30:3-5).

Pregnancy should not be the primary reason for marriage. Great strains are imposed on a forced marriage, making it much less secure than a normal marriage. Personally, I wish there were ways to make your boyfriend more responsible—financially, morally, and emotionally—for the baby he has fathered; but since it is so easy to get a divorce, forcing him to marry will not necessarily improve your situation. So why add the possibility of failure in marriage to all your other hurts? Why notch your self with another scar? Going through the motions of marriage vows never guarantees lasting love.

You are maybe wondering what your boyfriend will say when he finds out you are pregnant. I don't know what his specific answer will be, but I do know we are living in a time when a growing number of married men are opting for "freedom." After observing such an example, and not wanting to be "tied down," most teenage boys, when informed of their girlfriend's pregnancy, say, "Sorry, see you around." Nonetheless, there are legal means for getting child-support from the father.

Your boyfriend's response to your situation will determine how many options are still open to you. If he is still around and if you think you still *want* him to be around, then you have the option of talking with him about a future together. If at all possible, let both sets of parents have a part in these discussions.

What about living together? This option offers very little built-in security, because there is no such thing as a temporary *total* commitment. "Commit" means to give in trust, or surrender. Only marriage has that kind of quality. The marriage relationship cannot be "tried out," for marriage requires you to "burn your bridges behind you." Only this kind of commitment can provide security, in which feelings can be fully expressed and goals shared.

Living together is *not* the same as marriage. It isn't even close. It certainly isn't a substitute. If you aren't going to commit your lives to each other, then don't pretend in a live-in situation. You will be setting yourself and your baby up for more pain. People who have tried living together have told me, "What starts out as pure delight and contentment turns to guilt, anxiety, and depression."

Moving in together begins when two people say, "It feels good to be together"; or, "You turn me on, let's sleep together"; or, "I love you, let's get it on." To their disappointment, "making out" soon becomes as routine as eating pizza.

If you think you can build a relationship on the foundation called emotions or feelings, you must enjoy taking incredible risks! Thrills between two people come and go. If a permanent promise, a marriage commitment, does not exist between the two of you when the feelings begin to leave, your partner will also leave.

For many reasons we have become a "throwaway society." We discard Styrofoam cups and mates, having used them briefly.

Do you feel used? Bitter toward the father of the baby you are carrying? Bitter toward love?

So you wonder, what is love? If I don't live with or marry the father, will I ever be able to love again? Will any man ever accept and love me?

Sociologists define "love" as that relationship between two people which will lead to the optimum development of both. Would marriage to your boyfriend help each of you to develop your full potential?

You must think of as many aspects and angles as possible before you commit your life to marriage. If you don't, you are using as much sense as someone who jumps off a ship in the middle of the ocean without a life preserver.

Marriage can be a solution only if you are both willing and prepared to commit your lives fully to each other. It has to be all and always, or it is, in effect, nothing at all. Entering marriage with hesitation, or with self-centered love, or with reservation virtually guarantees failure.

In certain states, because of your age, marriage may not even be a legal option. These restrictions do not exist because some killjoy wanted to make your life miserable. Statistics show that if both partners are *under* twenty, the chance for a successful, lasting marriage is not nearly as good as if both partners are *over* twenty years of age. You are still growing and changing. If you marry now, you each may change in dissimilar ways, pursue different goals, and grow in opposite directions. Then one day you may wake up in bed with a husband who has become a stranger, and your marriage may become a divorce statistic.

If marriage is still a consideration for you, read the next few pages carefully. If marriage can't be a consideration, store the following information in your memory bank for the future.

Choosing a Husband

You need to understand what marriage is before it can become a solution. Many definitions exist, but most express the same basic ideas. Here are a few to ponder. See if they fit your relationship.

1. Marriage is a process, not a fulfillment.

2. Marriage is a joining together of two human lives whose goals are the *other's* growth and good. You may not do whatever pleases you. Your mate does not exist for you to use. You must share and sacrifice. You will want to be sensitive and concerned

for the welfare and happiness of someone other than yourself.

3. Marriage is a promise to love someone, even when you don't *feel* like it. Love is not "a special way of feeling," for feelings come and go. Love is an attitude and a choice.

4. Marriage is not so much a matter of finding the right person as *being* the right person for your partner.

5. Marriage is demanding. You have to work at love or it disappears.

6. Marriage requires continual commitment. (Stop! Memorize this rule. Maybe you should write it on a sheet of paper 100 times!) Commitment cements a marriage like Super Glue cements plastic.

It's important for you to know that every marriage partner comes "as is." So ask yourself, "What kind of person am I looking for? What are his priorities in life—are they similar to mine?" Also ask, "Can I love him without trying to change him?" In marriage you don't promise, "as long as we both shall *love*," but rather, "as long as we both shall *live*."

Picture each other with gray hair (or even no hair) and wrinkles. Ask each other, "What will you think of me when I look like that? Do you truly respect me and need me? Do we share a common purpose? Are you able to expose your secrets and dreams, unafraid that I will laugh? Are you proud of me?"

What are his skills? Can he support himself? Can he support you also? Can he support a *family*? (That's what your baby will make you.) Would you be able to establish a home financially? If he wants and needs to go to school, will you mind being left alone at home for many evenings? Will you mind being quiet so he can study? If you also want to go to school, are you each willing to live with a pinched budget? To share cooking, child care, washing and cleaning duties? To have very few nights out together, at least for a while?

Be *sure* of your decisions. Imagine all the complications and hard times *before* you get into a situation that you didn't expect and can't handle. Marriage will require sacrifice and hard work. But if you do it because you both really want to, you will love doing it together. For some, marriage is an option, but one which takes very careful thought and planning.

No matter what you decide about your relationship with your boyfriend, you will need to forgive him. It would be so easy for you to blame him, "*He* got me pregnant"—forgetting that you had a part in it, too. Don't resent him as the cause of your crisis. Don't hate him if he has left you to face this crisis alone. If you tolerate such feelings, they will grow and expand. Once out of control, they will harm you much more than they will ever affect him.

As you make this important decision about marriage, please remember to honor your parents by allowing them to take part in it. They want the best for you, so listen to them. Your pastor or another trusted counselor may also have wise insights for you as you face a choice which will affect *the rest of your life*—even more than your pregnancy.

4

THE ROSE BUD

"Should I Parent My Baby?"

Getting pregnant is really rather easy. Becoming a good parent is not. One teenage mother told me, "I didn't know it was going to be so hard raising a kid! Having to stay home all the time isn't much fun. Making ends meet is another problem. Welfare helps, but the baby's clothes and shoes cost so much. Sometimes I go without things I need in order to have enough money to buy all the milk and baby food she needs."

Just because you are pregnant does not mean you are ready to be a parent. You *do* have a choice—one of the most important you will ever make. Are you ready to be a parent? Should you parent your baby or place it for adoption? Your decision will affect the rest of your life.

The following questions are not a test. They do not have right or wrong answers. They are meant to help you judge whether or not you are prepared to be a parent. On a sheet of paper answer each question honestly, as it applies to you and your current situation. Answer yes or no, or give an explanation.

1. Do I enjoy children?

2. Have I ever cared for a child for twenty-four hours? A weekend? A week?

3. Am I patient enough to deal with the crying, noise, confusion and responsibility, day after day?

4. How do I act when I am angry or upset?

5. Would I take my feelings out on my child if I lost my temper?

6. What does "discipline" mean to me? (Setting limits? being strict? spanking? etc.)

7. Do I get along with my parents?

8. What will I do to avoid the child-raising mistakes my parents made?

9. How do I plan to take care of my child's health and safety?

10. Do I take care of my own health and safety?

11. Do I enjoy teaching others?

12. Am I a good communicator?

13. Am I able to tell others what I want, need or expect of them?

14. Would a child right now interfere with *my* growth and development?

15. Would raising a child right now change my educational plans?

16. Would I have the energy to go to school and raise a child at the same time?

17. Could I support a child financially?

18. Could I manage to raise a child and have the time and energy for a job?

19. Do I know how much physical and emotional energy it takes to raise a child? Do I "have what it takes"?

20. Would I be willing to cut back my social life and spend time with my child?

21. Would I be willing to give up the freedom to do what I want to do when I want to do it?

22. Would I miss my free time? My independence? My privacy?

23. *Am I willing to give the next eighteen or more years of my life to love and be responsible for my child, and to place concern for his or her well-being above my own?*

Your honesty as you answer these questions is critical. Your final decision is critical also. But what really matters is your *action* following this decision. Good intentions are wonderful, but you must also carry them out.

Raising a child will demand a lot of time. Many girls your age have developed very little understanding of normal infant behavior. Some would be unable to cope with the frustrations of having a small child. Child abuse is increasing and, unfortunately, is most common among teenage parents. Mistreatment and neglect often result from ignorance of the baby's needs.

It is not an automatic conclusion that because you are young you would do a poor job of raising your child. But your level of maturity is an important consideration. If you decide to keep the baby, your main career choice for the next eighteen years will be "motherhood." You will have to temporarily cancel any previous plans, working to gain skills and training for this long-term occupation. Mothering a little child is a huge responsibility. If you have never done it before, it may appear easy. After all, babies are so cute! We all love kittens, puppies, and lambs. None of these begin to compare with the love we feel for a newborn baby.

Unlike baby animals, however, human babies are helpless at birth. They are totally dependent on someone's constant attention, and they need care night and day. They are capable of crying nonstop for several hours (often in the middle of the night). When they are still very small, one of the first words they learn is "no." With that word comes the development of an independent will. They are not always well-behaved and lovable, and often choose to display this "other side" at the worst times—at the grocery store or in front of other people. They are always hungry. When you want to take them somewhere, they are asleep. They mess their pants—more than once a day. Without ever being taught, they can yell, stamp their feet, make a mess, be irritable....

If you choose to raise the child alone, how will you describe his father to him? Will you degrade him? Or will you make him out to be better than he was? Or will you talk about him honestly and constructively? Will your child be a constant reminder of your having been hurt by someone who got you pregnant and left?

If you sacrifice your future to raise your child, will you resent him and demand he repay your sacrifice the rest of his life? (It's hard to live with a martyr.)

Do your parents want to raise the child? Or have

you just assumed Mom and Dad will take on this responsibility for you? Have you thought about it from *their* viewpoint? How much would they have to give up if you brought a baby home to them? Are they approaching a time when they could be just a couple again, free from the heavy duties of child-rearing that have occupied their lives for many years already? Think of *their* feelings. Think of *their* needs and *their* marriage relationship.

Babies don't stay babies very long. The cute-and-cuddly stage is replaced quickly by the toddler-into-everything stage. Will your parents have to rearrange the house to make space for a growing little one? Are you asking your parents to share eighteen or more years of responsibility? Are you *sure* they want to do this? Are they ready and able to make such a commitment? Will they live long enough to see it through?

Three different generations in one home may cause friction. Who will be "in charge"? Will Grandma make all the decisions about the child, or will you? If your mother spends the most time mothering your child, how will you feel if the child eventually turns to *her* as "mother"? If you pursue new goals, want to get married, and/or move away, will the child move with you or stay with them? How will your parents feel about it? Might they even try to prevent that marriage because they fear losing "their" child? If you choose to parent your baby, talk with your parents about the problems you will face.

Have you considered your child's need for a *father?* We are living in a time when many girls choose not to marry their baby's father and try to raise their children alone. They argue that "men help make babies, that's all," or, "I can manage things just fine by myself," or, "Who needs a man?"

Listen carefully! Real men are more than baby makers. Even though you will spend the next nine months expecting a baby, when the baby is born, caring for your baby will be more than you expected! Raising your baby will be an even greater responsibility for you if you do not have a husband sharing it.

If you cannot give your child a good father, and if your answer to most of the questions at the beginning of this chapter was, "No, I'm not yet ready to be a parent," there is still one wonderful option open to you. Please consider *adoption*.

At this very moment, as you wonder whether you should parent your baby, a couple somewhere is waiting for the telephone to ring; one of tens of thousands of childless couples who have finished their education, have married, have established a home and are earning an adequate income, and are prepared and waiting to be parents. They are ready, willing, and eager to raise a child, but for a variety of reasons have not been able to conceive one. Since 1973, when abortion was legalized, there have been many fewer babies to adopt. Placing your baby for adoption, therefore, may be the very best solution for you, for your baby, and for some prepared couple.

Up until now we have spent some time together thinking about *you*: what's happening to *you*; what *you* think about things; how *you* feel; how *your* life has been interrupted and abruptly changed.

Now that you are pregnant, you must grow up fast and answer many "adult" questions: What is best for my baby's future? What is best for my parents, my family? What is best for the baby's father and his family? What is best for that couple who could offer a good home now and is waiting for a baby?

Put a wide-angle lens on your mental "camera" and view the "big picture"—the many people your decision will affect. Then, after much prayer and thought, do what seems best for *everyone*, under *all* the circumstances. It is possible that adoption may be the best solution.

You may not be aware of adoption procedures. The adoption process is not the same everywhere, so you will need to check the laws in your state for specific details. You can get answers to questions about the laws in your state from lawyers and the many agencies already mentioned that help pregnant girls.

The adoption process has two parts. Generally this is how it works.

1. You, the biological mother, must give consent for the baby to be adopted. Ask your counselor about state laws requiring the baby's father's consent.

2. A couple wanting to adopt a child must apply for adoption. A very thorough examination is made to ensure that these people will be good parents. They must meet certain basic adoption require-

ments, participate in interviews and take part in home studies.

Their age is considered. The couple must be old enough to establish a mature parent-child relationship but young enough to see a child through young adulthood.

Their ability to form warm, meaningful, lasting friendships, and to communicate will be checked through several personal references which the couple must provide.

The financial stability of the applicants is carefully considered. They must provide information about annual income, money-management skills, etc.

The health of the couple is checked; medical examinations are required to show if the couple is physically able to raise a child.

Many states require that a child be placed in a home of the same religious faith as his parents. All in all, the couple must prove they are prepared to provide a loving and stable home for your baby.

Once adoptive parents have been fully approved, and the required legal steps have been taken, you will sign a final consent form and the court will decree that the adoptive parents are legally responsible for the child.

Adoption can be arranged through an agency or it can be handled independently, sometimes called "private placement." Either way, the adoption procedures are determined by the laws of your state. Be careful not to get involved with a "baby broker" or a black-market adoption. You and your baby's rights and well-being will not be guarded if handled through these illegal transactions.

Planning adoption for your baby is a difficult choice. Just thinking about this choice may cause a flash-flood of feelings. Lots of questions follow: *Will my baby be okay? Will I wonder if I did the right thing? What am I going to feel like after I place the baby for adoption*—after a day ... after a week ... after a year? Will I have regrets? Will I feel empty and alone? Will I get depressed and grieve?

Some teenage girls who have already gone through this experience have offered their thoughts and feelings to help you know what to expect. You will probably be able to identify with some of their comments.

Suzie refused to rush into a forced marriage that she knew wouldn't work. She says, "Pregnancy would not have been a good reason for me to get married. The father didn't stay around. Forcing him to marry me wouldn't have been right. He would have been unhappy and then I would have been unhappy, and that would have affected the baby, too. I chose adoption because if the baby, when older, would start asking about his father, the questions would have been tough to handle. I would have felt resentful and I am sure the child would sense that. I know I did the right thing, but it was hard."

Lee says, "I knew it was not the right time for me to be a mother. Caring for a baby is a big responsibility. I was a junior in high school, and when I thought of the people who had waited years for a baby, people able to provide a good home right then, I knew I should place the baby for adoption."

Karen was only fourteen when she got pregnant and fifteen when her baby girl was born. She decided she wasn't old enough to be a parent, so she placed her newborn daughter for adoption. Karen says, "I knew it was the right thing to do, but panicky thoughts like, 'Should I try to keep her?' and, 'When she grows up, what will she think of me?' were there, too." Thoughtfully she continues, "The hardest time was when I had to go to the judge's chambers to sign the final papers. The judge asked, 'Do you know your rights are terminated?' I knew, and I cried. But I signed. I had to think about more than myself. I had to think about what was best for my baby."

Another girl has something she wants to say to you. Here is Cheryl's message:

"When the baby starts to move inside you, you'll go through a time when you think you *have* to keep it. Think about it really hard! You can't think of yourself. You must think of the baby. It isn't easy—but you'll know what you have to do. I knew I really loved the baby. I guess I placed her because I loved her so much."

Several of these girls feel strongly that they had a short, but very important, part in a long-term project.

Debbie says, "A lot of joy comes during a pregnancy that has nothing to do with keeping the baby or not. I'm just doing my best to take care of myself and make sure the baby will be healthy at birth. I will always remember I went through this, that I had the baby and gave him to someone. But that'll be easier than going through life remembering I had an abortion. It will be easier to think of a live child growing up with a family that really loves him than no child at all."

Patty says, "I never thought of the baby as mine. I thought of it as someone else's baby. He was mine for a few months, and was my responsibility then, but he was for someone else. I loved him and cared for him, for them. I've thought about it a lot. I know he has a good home. He needed two parents. Having a child, being a mother—I think of all that for the future. I'm looking forward to having a family someday, when the time is right."

Laura says she asked a friend of hers who had already had this experience, "What am I going to feel like after I place the baby for adoption? Will I have regrets?" Her friend replied, "I never forget the experience. I never forget the baby. Special days, such as birthdays and Mother's Day, always remind me." Laura added, "There will be problems either way. I decided it would be worse to ruin the child's life by keeping her. It isn't that I'm not loving her. It's *because* I love her so much."

Shelly did much serious thinking during her pregnancy and came to some firm conclusions. These were her words as she contemplated the birth of a child: "I expect some sorrow, but when I think of all the parents who give birth and the baby is stillborn, or dies shortly after birth, or has serious birth defects and what they have to go through. . . . I suppose I will go through periods of sadness for myself, but if the baby is okay, how can I really grieve?"

Placing your baby for adoption can be a very difficult decision. If you decide to do so, you can expect to feel many conflicting emotions—sorrow, depression and a sense of loss. They are natural feelings. Yes, you will no doubt wonder at times, *Did I do the right thing?* These doubts are normal. It will help if you admit your feelings to a trusted friend or counselor. Many adoption agencies offer professional counseling to pregnant girls, free of charge.

Are you wondering, *Should I see the baby and hold the baby before the separation takes place?* The answer is yes. Your natural curiosity will probably make you want to check and be sure he's okay. It will be healthy for you to see the baby as a separate person. This reality will help you as you begin to resolve the separation.

Many girls say they wrote a letter to the child, expressing their love and reasons for the decision. This was to be given to the child when the adoptive parents felt he would be old enough to understand.

A twelve-year-old boy who was adopted as an infant says, "I'm very grateful that my mother didn't abort me or try to raise me. She was eighteen and not married when I was born. It would have been hard to be raised by a lady who wasn't married. I'm glad she allowed me to be raised by a special family who love me."

Planning for your child to be part of an adoptive family is a mature action, based on selfless love. Every time doubts or regrets creep into your mind, remind yourself that you have placed your child's well-being above your own. Be proud.

If you have answered all the questions, carefully thought about your responses, and *still* don't have a clear answer, *don't panic.* There's still time to consider your own suitability for parenthood and to discuss it with caring people in your life.

On the other hand, don't put off your decision until after the baby is born. It should be made at a time when you are able to think clearly. Eventually even a nondecision becomes a decision, for your child could end up in foster-care, so don't drift through your pregnancy and your baby's birth without a clear plan.

And please remember that God loves and cares about you and your baby. He wants to help you make the best decision. There are many different ways that He can help you to know what you should do—through wise advice and counsel from family or friends, through circumstances, through reading the Bible, and through special insight He gives you deep inside. If you honestly ask God, "Should I parent my baby?" He will let you know the answer.

5

THE FLOWER OF
SELF-RESPECT

Growing in the Soil of God's Love

Many people today feel depressed and worthless. I would guess getting pregnant hasn't helped your self-image. In fact, it might be harder than ever to accept yourself now.

There are many reasons for feeling this way. Doubts about your measuring up probably began to sneak into your awareness years ago.

Before you were born, the "measuring" began. As your mother gained weight, everyone speculated and the doctor estimated your size. The day of your birth a nurse placed you on a scale alongside a yardstick and recorded your weight and length. When you were strong enough and able to stand, you climbed up on a jiggly scale and were told to stretch up tall while the nurse pulled a bar down on top of your head. Your growth was noted.

You were measured by new standards as you grew older—how fast you could run, how high you could jump, how many words you could spell. Upon entering the teenage years another measure gradually crept into your awareness. With statistics such as 5 feet and 36-24-36 came a sensitivity to what other people thought of you. You became hung up on how you looked and how you thought other people viewed you, so you began to build opinions of yourself. The Yardstick of Popular Opinion became important as you measured physical appearance, intelligence, athletic ability, clothes, car, boyfriends, etc. You know how they stack up in *your* life.

Have you ever met *anyone* who feels like a "10" in all these categories? Every year there's a new Miss America, a new valedictorian, a new athletic record, a new fashion fad, and a new model car. The standards keep changing. We all know how it feels not to quite measure up.

The inferior feelings come in a variety of packages. We set up unrealistic standards for ourselves, say these standards are what really matter, and then wonder why we fail. To further handicap ourselves, we practice self-criticism and self-condemnation. If we don't like ourselves very well, we will have difficulty accepting anyone else's compliments, evaluations or forgiveness. No wonder we feel inferior! We have allowed a false system of values to become our "ruler." We have compared ourselves to the wrong yardstick.

God offers a solution to this problem. It doesn't matter to Him how many/few hairs you have on your head; how many/few sweaters you own; how many/few words a minute you can type; how many/few people love you. God made you! You were created in *His* image. You are His "one-of-a-kind" creation. *Everything* He made was *good*— including you! Can you imagine the reputation He would earn if He ever made worthless junk?

God says you are priceless! He says you are at the top of His list. He placed the responsibility of taking care of you, His creation, into your hands. And He has blessed you with the knowledge of right and wrong and given you the freedom to choose.

So, how do we get messed up? Why do we sometimes feel so miserable? It's because we have broken our relationship with God. The cause is a three-letter word: S-I-N. Given the freedom to choose, we made the wrong choice!

Webster's dictionary defines sin as "willful violation of the divine laws—neglecting the laws of morality."

But it all seems so unfair! Everyone's "doing it," but you got caught! You could name lots of girls who are sleeping around, and maybe you did it only once. Yes, and your boyfriend did it too—but he isn't pregnant!

Listen. Getting "caught" isn't a sin. Being pregnant isn't a sin. It isn't even a punishment!

Being pregnant is a consequence of having sex. *Premarital sex* was the sin.

In this day and age I would be out on a limb sawing off the branch if *I* stood up on my own and said, "It's against the law to go to bed with your boyfriend." But there *is* such a law. The God who designed you said there are moral limits in relationships. He ought to know since He made us, and everyone should be paying better attention.

Such a law was given to us for our benefit, not because God is a spoilsport. The Bible is not the enemy of pleasure. Choosing to have sex and risk pregnancy probably gave you some pleasure. That's to be expected. After all, God made it to be fun. In fact, everything He made was *good*. Sex was meant to be wonderful. However, sex was not meant to be enjoyed until after certain commitments have been made between two people. True feelings of love can be fully expressed only within marriage, after a woman and man have resolved to make the relationship work and pledged themsleves never to call it quits.

Sometimes we try to cover up sin with other names so it won't seem so bad. But when we are all alone, and not making up excuses, we have to admit sin is sin and it is keeping us from a right relationship with God, with ourselves and other people.

The Bible is very clear that since the beginning, everyone has chosen to sin. If everybody sins, why do we feel guilty about it? What is guilt, anyway? God has built into every person a basic sense of right and wrong called conscience. When we choose what we know to be wrong, we feel uneasy inside. This affects our attitudes toward ourselves, toward others and especially toward God. That is guilt. Because of what we have done, because of the choices we have made, we are responsible. We can't blame someone else. No other person can *force* you to sin.

In a recent article in our newspaper, the author expressed surprise that in spite of all the sex education being taught in our schools today, teenagers still "feel guilty" after participating in premarital sex. I want you to know that you can never expect to feel any other way. The world will try to trick you into believing a lot of things that will harm you. To play around outside of God's moral law—and not expect to feel guilty or get hurt—is as ridiculous as it would be to jump out of a tree and expect to float to the ground and not be injured. We have to live with the consequences of our actions.

The universe in which we live is carefully ordered by God. If we break any of His established laws or try to change His order of things, the consequences become ours. Such dependable laws help to make life stable and predictable.

So what did God have in mind when He designed your conscience? The guilt feelings are signals to turn you away from whatever it was that turned them on in you. I can't tell you when to feel guilty. I don't need to! God will tap you on the shoulder when you are heading in the wrong direction. Don't ignore His warnings. Guilt feelings were meant to keep you out of trouble.

God's good news is that even though you ignored sin's "law of gravity," He doesn't leave you hurting in a heap under the tree. He loves you very much! He knows what the temptations to sin are, because, in Jesus Christ, He became man and felt the same temptations. God understands the pain of sin. And because He is God, He can help when you are hurting.

The Bible says, "He himself has shared fully in all our experience of temptation, except that He never sinned. Let us therefore approach the throne of grace with fullest confidence, that we may receive mercy for our failures and grace to help in the hour of need" (Heb. 4:15-16, Phillips).

According to Webster's dictionary, "grace" means "the unmerited favor and love of God toward you in Christ." None of us deserves it, but God offers it anyway. Christ, by dying on the cross, took the punishment for your sin. He opened your path to the Father by providing forgiveness. To receive forgiveness, you must admit to God you were wrong and be sorry for what you did.

God's great love for you certainly is reason enough for you to love yourself. He has made a huge investment in you. Never again think of yourself as worthless.

God knows how you got pregnant and everything else you have ever done. He knows all of your secret thoughts, ideas, wishes and dreams. Knowing, He still doesn't reject you. In fact, He insists that He loves you!

If you continue to feel guilty, you will destroy yourself. Guilt and depression are buddies. In order to stay alive, you need to breathe. In order to have a right relationship with God, you need to *accept* and *believe* God's forgiveness. He is waiting to give it to you. Stop right now and agree with God that you were wrong, that you need Him, and ask to be forgiven.

But don't stop there! Just as you need oxygen for physical life, you need the clean, pure air of forgiveness for your spiritual life. Receive the inward cleansing that God offers. It's the only way to really live.

Take a deep breath. Imagine God's life filling you the same way that the oxygen does. As you sit there, start digging your toes into the warm, soft soil of God's love. Plant yourself in it. Let your roots go down. Start to grow. And start to water this new plant with God's Word. To paraphrase the first Psalm, "Happy is the girl who ... enjoys reading the Bible.... She is like a flower that grows beside a stream; she gives fruit at the right time, and her leaves do not dry up. She succeeds in everything she does."

It's time to shake off the burden of comparison. Compete with yourself, not others. Improve your own record. Develop *your* own strengths. Honestly acknowledge your weaknesses and ask God to help you overcome them. The flower of self-respect will never grow in the soil of depression and despair.

Like a new plant, the new life God is beginning in you must be nourished and encouraged to grow. Make sure you do the following:

1. Make a daily appointment with God and then keep it.

2. Read a few verses from your Bible. Write down what you have learned.

3. Take time to pray. Talk over your day with God.

4. Spend some time with at least one other person who knows Him, too. If you do not have a church, find one to attend.

5. Look around for someone who has needs and see what you can do to help. Giving love to someone else will do wonders for how you feel about yourself.

6. Take ten minutes and write your answer to the question, "Who am I?" You can start with your name and a few facts about yourself, but try to go deeper. Who are you *really*? The next few pages are a do-it-yourself kit to help you discover more about yourself.

"Who Am I"

Is it hard to answer the question, "Who am I?" Many times we don't know who we are at all, so we spend a great deal of time trying to establish an "identity." We look in many directions for an identity that we will like.

We sometimes try to define ourselves by our *activities.* We place great emphasis on what we do at school, at work, or on other interests. We stay busy, busy, busy. "Who am I? I am all these activities!"

We also try to define ourselves by our *appearance.* We spend lots of time trying to get a certain "look." We work on our skin, our hair, our weight and our clothes. We try to own the right things. "Who am I? I am how I look to myself and to other people."

Or we try to define ourselves by our *relationships.* "I am who I know—my friends and my family."

We also attempt to define ourselves by our talents, dreams, fears, failures, thoughts, experiences, personality, characteristics and habits.

Did you include any of these areas in your answer to the question, "Who am I?" It's not surprising that we're often confused about our identity. When anything goes wrong in one or more of these areas (and it frequently does), we often feel pretty bad about ourselves. It's easy to feel worthless when we don't like our looks, when our activities don't seem to be very important, when our relationships are rocky, and when we don't like our personality. Yes, it's easy to feel like a failure.

But what does God think of us? When you stop to think about it, how God feels about us is what really matters. Since He is our creator, He knows who we are. Let's look at some Bible passages to see what God says.

I Am Understood by God!

Read Psalm 139. (The Psalms are found in the middle of the Bible.)

1. What are some of the characteristics of God that David describes in this psalm?
2. David says that God knows everything about him, and that there is no place where he can hide from God. How does David respond to this? Why do you think he feels this way?
3. How do you feel about being thoroughly known and understood by God? (Thankful? Afraid?

Ashamed? Secure? Insecure? Joyful?) Why do you feel this way?

4. One reason David delights in being known by God is that he is confident that God loves, understands, protects and guides him (see vv. 5, 10, 14, 17, etc.). In the same way, God cares about you (1 Pet. 5:7). What is one area of your life you would like to hide from God (as in v. 7)? What is one area of "darkness"—of trouble—(as in v. 11) that threatens to hide you from God?

5. Write a short letter to God about the area of your life that is a little hard to talk about with Him. What kind of letter do you think He would want to write you in return?

I Am Not Junk!

1. How would you describe God's relationship with David, as described in Psalm 139? How long has God been a part of David's life?

2. How does David describe the process of his own creation?

3. How do you think David might answer the question, "Who am I?"

4. David praises God for having created him (v. 14). Why?

5. How do you feel about God's creation of you? What part of you do you have a hard time accepting as being "fearfully and wonderfully made"?

6. Write out verses 13 and 14 on a card and tape them to your mirror. Say these verses to yourself

each time you look in the mirror during the next week (or more!).

I Am Forgiven

Read 1 John 1:5-2:2 (toward the end of the Bible and different than the *Gospel* of John).

1. What is God like, according to this passage?
2. What makes it so difficult for people to have fellowship with Him?
3. What is God's answer to this difficulty?
4. What is our responsibility in all of this?
5. What does "walking in the light" mean to you?
6. The Good News takes effect when we quit pretending that we're good, and instead take our sins to God to be forgiven. What are some things that keep you from "walking in the light"? Why not talk to God about these things right now?

David wrote Psalm 51 as his confession during a very hard time in his life. You might want to read it. At another time David wrote Psalm 32, which tells of other times when God forgave him. Paul wrote in 1 Timothy 1:12-16 about being forgiven; there he calls himself the "worst of sinners." Read carefully and meditate on 1 Timothy 1:15 and 16 (this book of the Bible comes a little before 1 John).

You are forgiven! God forgives you because Christ died for you. That's good news! But the problem is learning to forgive yourself. Satan accuses you over and over, and your mind and heart don't forget easily. Yet God says you're forgiven. So whom are you going to believe? If God has forgiven, do you dare to condemn yourself any longer? "There is therefore now no condemnation to them who are in Christ Jesus" (Rom. 8:1).

I Am Loved!

Read Romans 8:28-39 (in the middle of the New Testament).

1. What are some of the things that God has done for us?
2. Paul asks in verse 31, "What then shall we say to these things? If God is for us, who is against us?" How does Paul answer his own question in the next verses?
3. How would *you* answer Paul's question? Make a list of some of the people or circumstances that are against you right now. How would Paul respond to each of them?
4. Have you ever wondered whether anybody really loves you? How would Paul answer that feeling?
5. For what problem do you need to know God's love for you right now? Write verses 37-39 and make your own list.
6. If you truly believe that God loves you as much as He says He does, how do you think this next week will be different for you?

Have you ever been in love? Do you remember how you felt (or feel) about the one you loved? Consider this: God loves you far more than that! John 3:16 says, "God so loved the world [and that includes each of us], that He gave His only begotten Son, that whoever believes in Him should not perish, but have eternal life." God loves you so much He can't take His eyes off you! (You could tape that sentence to your mirror, too.)

Now ask yourself again, "Who am I?" Who you think you are will color how you live. If you define yourself by your activities, by your relationships, by your appearance, by your personality, or by your fears, dreams, experiences and failures, you will often end up disliking yourself very much. But God has another view of you which is *true* and *unchanging*. He says that you are a unique, unrepeatable miracle of His creation; that you are known and understood fully; and that if you have confessed and repented, you are forgiven completely; you are loved no matter what—all because of what He has done for you through His Son, Christ Jesus. You are a child of the King of the universe; you are a beloved one; you are His personal concern.

A prominent Swiss businessman who had been successful and honored in many ways was once asked, "Just who are you?" Quietly and without any hesitation he answered, "I am a man with a friend. That is all that I am—but that is everything, for His name is Jesus."

6

THE ROSE BUSH

How to Care for *You*

When someone gives you a rose bush, the gift usually comes with instructions entitled, "How to Care for Your Rose Bush." Inside you'll find guidelines for proper temperature, watering, fertilizer, etc.

You are much more important than a plant. Now that you are carrying a child, you must work extra hard to maintain good health. It won't just "happen." If you follow carefully the guidelines in this chapter, they will help you achieve good health and be physically and emotionally strong through these important months of your life.

Medical Care

As early as possible, you should start seeing a professional regularly: a doctor, licensed nurse, or midwife. He/she will monitor your health and your baby's development. If any problems arise, they will be diagnosed and corrected. At first you will be checked about once a month. Later, your appointments will be more often. During the last month, you will be checked weekly.

Most communities have childbirth preparation classes. Don't worry—there will be other single mothers in the classes. Maybe your mom or a friend would be able to attend with you. Call a local hospital, clinic or appropriate social service agency for information. Many community colleges also offer these courses.

Diet

Usage has changed the meaning of "diet." The word makes most of us think of crash programs, weight loss and general starvation. Actually, diet means "to eat according to prescribed rules for health's sake." And in your case, you must eat nutritiously.

Depending on your size, you should gain an average of almost 3 pounds for each month of your pregnancy, or between 20 and 30 pounds. However, the largest share of your weight gain will occur in the last half of the pregnancy, so go easy at first.

Your doctor no doubt will caution you not to gain too much weight. Unnecessary pounds will increase the chance of complications. And being overweight won't help you feel very good about yourself. Your doctor also will tell you how much weight you should gain, depending on your "starting size." If you are now overweight, don't cut calories and lose weight until after the baby is born, or you will risk short-changing the nutritional needs of your growing child. If you are under seventeen, *you* are also growing and developing, and have your own set of needs.

If you are underwieght, your pregnancy will add to your body's needs. Therefore, eat with good health in mind.

The following guide to good nutrition during pregnancy is recommended by the National Research Council. Since each woman's needs are different, use it only as a *general* guide. If you have specific questions jot them down in a notebook and discuss them during your next visit with your doctor.

Foods To Be Eaten Daily

Milk—one quart of whole milk, or skimmed milk for weight control. Skimmed milk powder may be used as a substitute for, or supplement to, liquid milk (e.g., 1-2 tablespoons added to one glass of milk). One ounce of cheddar cheese may be substituted for one glass of milk.

Eggs—at least one daily.

Meat—six to eight ounces of lean meat (beef, veal, lamb, chicken, turkey or fish), preferably in two servings. Organ meats (liver, kidney) may be substituted twice weekly.

Fat—up to two tablespoons of butter, margarine or vegetable oil each day.

Bread—two slices of whole grain or enriched bread, plus a half cup of enriched or cooked whole grain cereal (one extra slice of bread may be substituted for cereal).

Vegetables—(a) potato, one medium (¾ cup of cooked rice, noodles, spaghetti, or macaroni may be substituted twice weekly); (b) dark green or deep yellow vegetable, average one cup; (c) one other vegetable, raw or cooked, average one cup, except peas, beans, corn, lentils, beets (½ cup).

Fruit—(a) citrus fruit (2 oranges or 1 grapefruit), or 8 oz. of citrus fruit juice (8 oz. of tomato juice may be substituted for one orange, one-half grapefruit or four oz. citrus fruit juice); (b) one other fresh fruit or one-half cup cooked or unsweetened fruit. Prunes (4-5) or dried apricots (5-6) may be used.

Basic Eating Guide

1. Enjoy a good balanced diet. Check what you eat with the above Nutrition Guide.
2. Drink six to eight glasses of water every day, between meals.
3. Be grateful for your food. Before each meal, pause and give thanks to God, asking Him to bless it for you and your baby's bodily needs.
4. If you are angry, tense or under emotional stress, *don't* eat. Wait a while until you are able to simmer down.
5. Eat slowly and enjoy your food. You won't eat as much and will feel better when you are through.
6. Avoid going back for seconds.
7. Avoid skipping meals and filling up on junk foods. In fact, avoid junk food!
8. Eat proper portions of quality food.
9. Avoid heavy consumption of some soft drinks (including the diet type), coffee (the worst offender), tea and cocoa. Their high caffeine content may

cause a baby to have low birth weight and even mild brain damage which may later cause learning disabilities.

10. Do not smoke, drink alcohol, or take any drugs/medications without your doctor's permission.

11. Avoid salty foods, especially in the last three months of your pregnancy.

Unfortunately, heartburn often occurs in pregnancy. Certain foods will increase this problem. Avoid spicy or deep-fried foods and most sweets—especially sweets on an empty stomach. Sometimes yogurt (frozen yogurt tastes great!) or buttermilk will make you feel better.

Bad eating habits and poor nutrition may cause your skin to become dull and blemished and your hair to lose its luster. Your fingernails may break easily and you may feel tired and listless. You may feel depressed, nervous or even grouchy. So, you see, it's really important to eat quality calories (skip the empty ones). And forget the saying, "If a little is good, a lot would be better." Eat sensibly.

Exercise

Your body *wants* to feel good! Your muscles were made to move. Moderate exercise will be good for you. In general, you should continue with your routine activities. It's better *not* to start new and strenuous sports. Swimming is excellent. If you play tennis, keep doing it. Ride your bicycle. Unless you've been doing it regularly, don't start jogging. Avoid hot tubs and saunas. Above all, don't let yourself get too tired.

If you are not very athletic, try walking every day. Walk at least a mile within a period of twenty to thirty minutes. You may need to work up to this gradually. Walking will strengthen and condition key muscles and will stimulate your cardiovascular system (heart, lungs and blood vessels). Fitness depends upon *faithfully* following an exercise program. Exercise can't be stored.

Be sure to stop *any* activity when you are tired. Some girls find they need a midafternoon nap. Make an effort to get enough rest. You *and* your baby will be in trouble if you don't. Dark circles under the eyes and a lifeless-looking, pale complexion will give you away; and your energy level and disposition will be very low if you don't exercise. If you sometimes can't sleep, try relaxing in a warm shower and then fix a warm milk drink just before climbing into bed. Reading helps some people fall asleep.

Drugs

Be careful about using any drugs—even over-the-counter types. Don't take *any* medication, any pills, without first asking your doctor, no matter how harmless it may seem. Nearly all drugs pass through the placenta to the baby. Some collect there, building up in higher concentration than in you, the mother. There are so many "unknowns" regarding drugs, and yet so much is at stake!

One doctor says, "The best advice I can give you about drugs when you're pregnant is don't expose yourself to the unknown. If you wouldn't give the drug to a baby, you probably shouldn't be taking it yourself."

Another doctor cautions against: taking medicines (unless prescribed), smoking, drinking *any* alcohol, radiation directly to the stomach (even dental X-rays are not advised), and exposure to infection, particularly venereal disease. Any one of these can lead to abnormal fetal development.

Certain drugs are likely to kill the embryo in the first few days of pregnancy. After the eleventh day they may cause birth defects. It's all in the combinations and timing. Let your doctor decide about tranquilizers, sedatives, laxatives, nosedrops, antihistamines, cold tablets, weight-control pills, pain pills, etc. Avoid hormones (even cortisone creams for your skin), antithyroid drugs, streptomycin, tetracyclines and anticoagulants. This is serious business!

Any drug, no matter how it is administered, can get through to your baby. Even aspirin can be harmful. Drugs that comfort you may play havoc with your baby's development. Let the professionals do their job as they provide the best possible care for both of you. Your doctor will know if you should take an antibiotic to control an infection (sometimes certain prescribed drugs will be very *necessary* to your health).

If you are eating a variety of healthy foods, you will probably be fine. If your doctor notices a deficiency, he will prescribe vitamin and/or iron supplements, according to your needs. Use *only* prescribed or approved vitamins or minerals. Guessing games can be dangerous. A vitamin imbalance can muddle your whole system. Certain vitamins, in excess, may harm you and/or your baby.

If you should happen to be one of the many (50-60%) pregnant women who experience some degree of nausea (better known as "morning sickness" because it happens most often first thing in the morning—but it can occur at any time during the day), talk to your doctor. Some fortunate people never experience this. It ordinarily takes about twelve weeks for a woman's body to adjust to the many hormonal changes that are taking place. Sometimes, what you eat (or smell) will bring on the upset, and sometimes it won't matter what you eat; you'll just feel horrible.

No one knows for sure what causes this problem, but it seems to have something to do with low blood sugar. Therefore, don't let yourself go too long without eating so you get too hungry. Even if you don't feel an appetite for food, a small, high-protein meal may help. Because it's a long time between dinner and breakfast, some girls keep dry crackers beside the bed and eat them before rising in the morning. Certain anti-nausea medications have been linked to birth defects, so don't take any morning sickness medicine unless your doctor prescribes it for you.

If you think you need a laxative (iron supplements can constipate), try bran cereal, raw vegetables and fresh fruits first. If your problem persists, consult your doctor.

According to the American Medical Association, smoking is injurious to your health. If you are pregnant, smoking can also harm your baby. Nicotine constricts your blood vessels, thus reducing the flow of blood—and oxygen and nutrients—to the placenta and the baby; this stunts growth and may deprive the baby of adequate nutrition. Pregnant women who smoke heavily tend to have small babies. Statistically, low birth weight babies are more apt to have learning problems later than those with average birth weight.

It is even possible that a mother's smoking will produce long-term, deeply rooted anxiety in an unborn child which will remain with him at birth. Studies show that an unborn baby becomes emotionally agitated (measured by his heartbeat) every time a mother even *thinks* of having a cigarette. Because smoking lowers the baby's oxygen supply, he anticipates the unpleasant sensations it will produce in him. This places him in a chronic state of fear and uncertainty which may predispose him to a lifetime of conditioned anxiety. Beware!

A pregnant woman who drinks alcohol risks having a child with birth defects. Mental retardation, hyperactivity, heart murmur and facial deformities are some of the possibilities. This isn't new. Even the Greeks and Romans noticed that mothers who were drinkers bore a greater percentage of sickly and deformed babies. New studies show that as few as two drinks a day may cause some neurological (nervous system) damage to the baby. Most doctors feel that it is best to avoid alcohol totally during pregnancy.

Finances

I'm sure by now you have thought, "How am I going to pay for everything?" Some families have medical insurance that will cover doctor and hospital fees. There are also welfare programs which can help. A counselor from one of the agencies listed on pages 88-94 will be able to advise you.

If you have a job, I encourage you to keep working as long as you feel up to it. There are laws which protect the employment of pregnant women if the activity does not harm her or her baby.

Even if you have decided not to marry the father of your child, he can be held legally responsible for medical and child-support costs. Again, a trained counselor can give you the details on procedures in your state.

Hospital

Your doctor or health care professional will be happy to lay out the options for the care you will need when it is time for your baby to be born. Jot down any questions you may have between now and your next visit. Your doctor may *assume* you have a clear picture of what will happen and when, so feel free to ask for details.

If your baby will be born in a hospital and you decide to have him adopted, there may be certain procedures that should be clarified beforehand. For instance, if you have decided to see and hold your baby during the hospital stay, your doctor may need to instruct the hospital staff accordingly. Your counselor will be able to help you think of arrangements which should be made ahead of time.

Mental Attitude

We know so much more about pregnancy than we did even a few years ago, which is certainly to your advantage. We now know that your baby can see, hear, taste, move deliberately, and even remember or learn in your uterus *before* he is born. The most exciting news is that he can *feel* emotions! Your baby is mentally aware, and because he is, what happens to him during the nine months that you are carrying him will shape and mold his emotional development—good or bad. Your tools for aiding this process are *your thoughts and feelings.* What you think about your child during the next few months will make an important difference.

What a child feels and perceives will begin shaping his attitudes and expectations. The "messages" you give him in the womb will affect his life to some degree. You can help him be happy or sad, aggressive or meek, secure or full of anxiety. Though God makes each person responsible for his own life, there is no doubt that your attitude can partially shape the personality and general well-being of your child.

You might wonder, *How does my baby know he is loved?* Since he really can hear you, one way is to talk to him. If your voice sounds soft and soothing and kind, he will feel loved and wanted. Recent studies show the baby hears clearly and even moves his body in rhythm to your speech.

Even a four-month-old baby in the womb will respond to sound, melody and rhythm. This new finding came as no surprise to me. My daughter, Sarah, communicated likes and dislikes in music long before she was born. She did not like loud music with a heavy beat, and she moved or kicked in protest. On the other hand, she relaxed and we both rested when I softly sang lullabies and rocked in a chair in a quiet room.

We all know how nice it is to be touched in a positive, reassuring way. Try gently stroking your tummy when your baby is disturbed and moving a lot. Accompany your actions with reassuring words—"That's okay. Everything is fine."

When you realize that what you *think* about your child—love, rejection, ambivalence—is shaping his future emotional life, his self-esteem and sense of security, you will begin to realize your awesome responsibility. What matters most is how you *feel* toward your baby. Your attitude has an enormous affect on how he will view life. He can't cope with a relentless assault of negative or anxious feelings from you.

Include your baby in your life and he will thrive. And so will you. You won't feel so lonely. When you forget yourself and try to help someone else (your baby), you will quickly feel better also! It will certainly benefit your baby.

You will have occasional fears, twinges of uncertainty and doubt. You will wonder how you look—your changing figure may worry you. You will have pressure from school assignments and financial needs. All of these problems are normal. They will *not* damage your child.

What are you expecting? Every pregnant woman goes through physical, mental, and emotional changes. They are *normal.* You may *feel* abnormal, but even *that's* normal. These changes may cause temporary discomfort. That's to be expected. And things such as an enlarged rib cage and breasts, stretch marks, and the dark line trailing down from your navel don't help you feel very beautiful. I don't know about you, but personally, I can withstand a lot of discomforts if I know they won't last forever. During the final few weeks you may feel clumsy as an elephant as you carry around what has become quite a load. But keep in mind that you are bringing forth a new life—filled with potential. That will help make this a very satisfying experience.

The dictionary defines *pregnant* this way: "being with young; *full of importance, full of significance.*" You are living in the middle of one of the most important and significant times in you life. Give it your best! Feel good physically and feel good emotionally. Decide now to make the most of the days ahead.

You are investing part of your life in a project that is beyond yourself: the birth of a child. The project will affect you in many ways. Your feelings and attitudes and understanding will grow and stretch right along with your tummy. At times you will feel strong, weak, terrified, bewildered and confident—sometimes all at once.

The Apostle Paul wrote to his friends at Colossae some words that will especially help you during this time: "... we haven't stopped praying for you and asking God to fill you with a clear knowledge of His will by giving you every kind of spiritual wisdom and understanding so that you live worthy of the Lord, aiming to please Him in every way as you produce every kind of good work and grow by knowing your God better. *We ask Him according to His wonderful might to strengthen you with all the power you* need to endure patiently whatever comes" (Col. 1:9-11, Berkeley trans.).

7

THE MASTER FLORIST

Help for the Future

"Keep your face to the sunshine and you cannot see the shadow."—Helen Keller

Pregnancy has a beginning and an end. As surely as you got pregnant, the day will come when you can see your feet again! The old expression "a watched pot never boils" means that when you are waiting for something, it seems like it will never happen. So as your pregnancy drags on, set your mind on other things and keep active. Your attitude will make all the difference.

Sometimes, even when you are surrounded by people, you will feel very alone. You may think you will be happier if you go away from home. Or if you do move away, you may think you would have been happier if you could have stayed at home. Remember, wherever you go, you take *yourself* with you! There is a lot to live for, and someday when you look back you will realize these nine months weren't so long after all.

Why not consider each day that comes as a "mini-lifetime"? What seems impossible to do for your whole pregnancy can be done for a single day. Do you think you have enough courage to meet the scary situations and rise above these fears—just for today? Could you set out to learn something new and share it with someone—just for today? Could you put forth the effort to smile and give happiness to others—just for today? Whatever you face that seems difficult, could you face it *a day at a time?*

If you fail one day, ask God to forgive you. Then forgive yourself, too. Over a hundred years ago, Emerson wrote, "Finish every day and be done with it. Tomorrow is a new day."

As you begin to live each new day, remember this: even though you aren't a virgin anymore, you are forgiven. Jesus once talked to a girl who had just been caught sleeping with a man who wasn't her husband. He told her, "I don't condemn you either. . . . Go, *from now on don't sin anymore*" (John 8:11, Berkeley trans.). I must caution you that once you have experienced this warm, intimate relationship, you may long for it again. Don't be surprised by new temptation to have premarital intercourse. Be prepared for those overwhelming feelings and do everything you can to avoid repeating your mistake.

As you have certainly noticed, this is not a book of answers. Rather, it's a book full of questions. Life is full of questions and options. The major question you must answer is not, "Should I keep my baby?" The most important question you will ever answer is: *Will I let Jesus Christ be the Lord [master] of my life?"* God, the Master Florist, offers a complete solution to all of your days ahead—far beyond the days of your pregnancy. When He is in charge, He will show you, step by step, what you should do. He will give you specific answers through the Bible, through other people who know Him, and through your conscience. Like a flower, open yourself to Him and allow Him to arrange your life in every detail.

"Do not call to mind the former things, or ponder things of the past. Behold, I will do something new . . . Will you not be aware of it?" (Isa. 43:18, 19).

When you fall asleep tonight, this day will be over. One day you will wake up and your pregnancy will be over, too.

Tomorrow is a new day. . . . Rejoice and be glad in it!

A FINAL NOTE

Dear Reader:

It would seem easy for me, in a detached manner, to write many profound statements telling you what to do or what not to do as a pregnant teenager. However, I have a sixteen-year-old daughter who is also a precious friend. Therefore, I have personally struggled with the thought, *What if you were my daughter?* I have wondered, *How easy would it be for me to support her through nine embarrassing and uncomfortable months? After delivery, could I allow this grandchild to go into an adoptive family?*

Everything I have told you, I believe to be true. There are no *easy* answers. However, some choices are definitely better than others! I hope I have convinced you to choose *life* for your baby and helped you to look at the options before you. Most of all, I hope I have encouraged you to turn to your Heavenly Father. *Should you keep your baby?* He will help you decide.

Having written to you, I will never be the same. Needless to say, I will be praying—I'm not just saying this to make you feel better. Prayer is a miracle! Every morning when I pray, God will know who you are, where you are and what you need. Remember, God promises to love you, no matter what. When some of the rest of us aren't there, or if we fall apart and fail, God is still with you. Trust Him to take care of you and your baby.

"... But one thing I do, forgetting what lies behind and straining forward to what lies ahead, I press on toward the goal for the prize of the upward call of God in Christ Jesus" (Phil. 3:13, 14, RSV).

CRISIS PREGNANCY CENTERS OF THE CHRISTIAN ACTION COUNCIL

ARIZONA

Phoenix
Crisis Pregnancy Center
602-945-6455

Tucson
Crisis Pregnancy Center
602-326-2263

CALIFORNIA

Mountain View
Santa Clara County CPC
408-730-2238

Pacifica
Crisis Pregnancy Center
415-355-0760

Pacific Grove
Give Life a Chance CPC
408-394-4590

Santa Cruz
CPC of Santa Cruz
408-458-3335

Union City
East Bay CPC
415-487-HELP

COLORADO

Denver
Denver CPC
303-759-2965

Greeley
Greeley CPC
303-353-2673

DELAWARE

Newark
New Castle County CPC
302-366-0285

FLORIDA

Gainsville
Crisis Pregnancy Center
904-377-4947

GEORGIA

Augusta
Greater Augusta CPC
404-724-5531

INDIANA

Indianapolis
Central Indiana CPC
317-243-6202

KENTUCKY

Murray
Lifehouse
502-753-0700

MARYLAND

Baltimore
Greater Baltimore CPC
301-243-6666

Bowie
Bowie CPC
301-262-1330

MICHIGAN

Sault Ste. Marie
Crisis Pregnancy Center
906-635-1103

MINNESOTA

Minneapolis
New Life CPC
612-920-1006

Pine City
Pine City CPC
612-629-2792

NORTH CAROLINA

Charlotte
Charlotte CPC
704-372-5981

NEW HAMPSHIRE

Hanover
Crisis Pregnancy Center
603-448-5373

NEW JERSEY

Plainfield
Crisis Pregnancy Center
201-968-3844

Princeton
Alpha Pregnancy Center
609-921-0494

NEW MEXICO

Gallup
Gallup CPC
505-722-4713

NEVADA

Lake Tahoe
High Sierra CPC
916-577-5373

OHIO

Ashland
Ashland CPC
419-281-1111

Dayton
Dayton CPC
513-296-0173

PENNSYLVANIA

Allentown
Lehigh Valley CPC
215-821-4000

Erie
Pregnancy Aid Center
814-459-4050

Philadelphia
Alpha CPC
215-546-8686

cont. on next page

VIRGINIA

Richmond
Richmond CPC
804-272-8111

Roanoke
Crisis Pregnancy Center
703-343-9596

WASHINGTON

Renton
Crisis Pregnancy Center
206-255-4544

WISCONSIN

Eau Claire
Apple CPC
715-834-7734

BETHANY CHRISTIAN SERVICES

24-hour Crisis Pregnancy Hotline—1-800-BETHANY

CENTRAL OFFICE

901 Eastern Avevue, N.E.
Grand Rapids, MI 49503
616/459-6273

CALIFORNIA

115D Mark Randy Place
Modesto, CA 95350
209/522-5121

COLORADO

Suite 210
2150 So. Bellaire St.
Denver, CO 80222
303/758-4484

IOWA

322 Central Ave. N.W.
P.O. Box 143
Orange City, IA 51041
712/737-4831

MARYLAND

The Farmhouse
500 Wilson Road
Annapolis, MD 21401
301/266-5381

MICHIGAN

6995 West 48th St.
P.O. Box 173
Fremont, MI 49412
616/924-3390

135 North State Street
Zeeland, MI 49464
616/772-9195

MISSOURI

7750 Clayton Rd.
St. Louis, MO 63117
314/644-3535

NEW JERSEY

475 High Mountain Road
North Haledon, NJ 07508
201/427-2566

PENNSYLVANIA

906 Bethlehem Pike
Suite 206
Erdenheim, PA 19118
215/233-4626

SOUTH CAROLINA

300 University Ridge
Suite 114
Greenville, SC 29601
803/235-2273

TENNESSEE

4706 Brainerd Rd.
Cha-Vira Plaza, Suite 104
Chattanooga, TN 37411
615/622-7360

NATIONAL COMMITTEE FOR ADOPTION

Suite 326
1346 Connecticut Ave., N.W.
Washington, D.C. 20036
202/463-7559

National Adoption Hotline:
202/463-7563

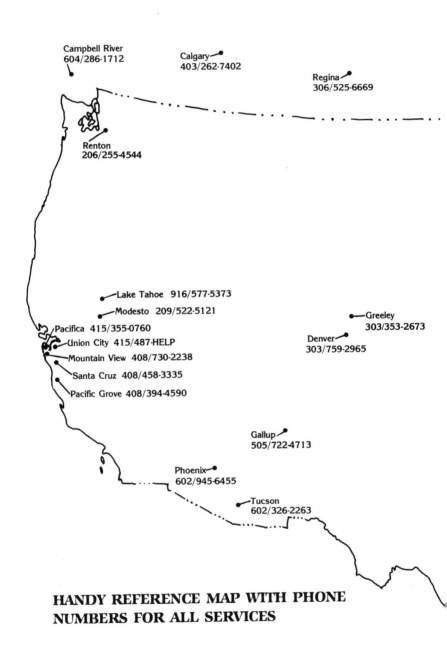

Campbell River
604/286-1712

Calgary
403/262-7402

Regina
306/525-6669

Renton
206/255-4544

Lake Tahoe 916/577-5373

Modesto 209/522-5121

Greeley
303/353-2673

Pacifica 415/355-0760

Union City 415/487-HELP

Denver
303/759-2965

Mountain View 408/730-2238

Santa Cruz 408/458-3335

Pacific Grove 408/394-4590

Gallup
505/722-4713

Phoenix
602/945-6455

Tucson
602/326-2263

**HANDY REFERENCE MAP WITH PHONE
NUMBERS FOR ALL SERVICES**

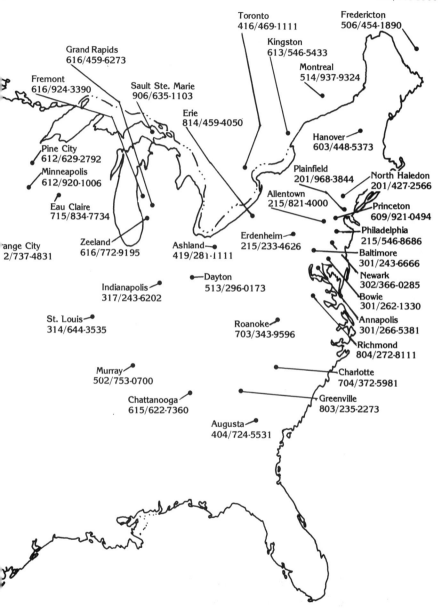

Antigonish
902/863-3300

Toronto
416/469-1111

Fredericton
506/454-1890

Kingston
613/546-5433

Montreal
514/937-9324

Grand Rapids
616/459-6273

Fremont
616/924-3390

Sault Ste. Marie
906/635-1103

Erie
814/459-4050

Hanover
603/448-5373

Pine City
612/629-2792

Minneapolis
612/920-1006

Plainfield
201/968-3844

North Haledon
201/427-2566

Allentown
215/821-4000

Princeton
609/921-0494

Eau Claire
715/834-7734

Philadelphia
215/546-8686

ange City
2/737-4831

Zeeland
616/772-9195

Ashland
419/281-1111

Erdenheim
215/233-4626

Baltimore
301/243-6666

Newark
302/366-0285

Dayton
513/296-0173

Bowie
301/262-1330

Indianapolis
317/243-6202

Annapolis
301/266-5381

St. Louis
314/644-3535

Roanoke
703/343-9596

Richmond
804/272-8111

Murray
502/753-0700

Charlotte
704/372-5981

Chattanooga
615/622-7360

Greenville
803/235-2273

Augusta
404/724-5531

CANADIAN BIRTHRIGHT CENTERS

NATIONAL OFFICE

777 Coxwell Ave.
Toronto, Ont. M4C3C6
416/469-1111

ALBERTA

203 333-17th Ave. S.W.
Calgary, Alb. T2S0A7
403/262-7402

BRITISH COLUMBIA

414-1180 Ironwood St.
Campbell River, B.C. V9W5P7
604/286-1712

NOVA SCOTIA

St. Francis Xavier University
Antigonish, N.S. V2G1X0
902/863-3300

NEW BRUNSWICK

621 Churchill Rd.
Fredericton, N.B. E3D1P5
506/454-1890

ONTARIO

Box 1052
Kingston, Ont. K7L4Y5
613/546-5433

QUEBEC

1800 Dorchester St. W.
Montreal, Que. H3H2HZ
514/937-9324

SASKATCHEWAN

105-1855 Scarph
Regina, Sask.
306/525-6669

A LETTER TO PARENTS

Dear Parents:

You and your daughter now face a crisis everyone dreads, an unplanned pregnancy. It's one thing to read about other people's problems, but quite another when your daughter becomes one of the "statistics."

At first, your thoughts may be racing to find someone to blame in order to ease the pain: *Why did you let this happen to us, God?* or, *The minute he walked through the door, I knew . . . ;* or, *If only her father had spent more time with her.*

We are complex creatures, so there were probably many reasons and circumstances that led to this situation. The simple truth is, your daughter probably thought she was in love at the time.

Since you can't change the past, the sooner you move through this stage of emotion, the better for you and your daughter. Pour your energy into helping her now. Even though you feel terrible, the world hasn't come to an end. Let her know your real feelings—that you are sad, concerned, shocked. Go ahead and cry with her. But don't push her into a corner with no way out. Encourage your daughter; let her know you are willing to uphold her as she carries the baby to term. Abortion may seem a simple way out, but the memory and its destructive effects last for a lifetime. At this moment you probably don't know what the resolution of your daughter's situation will be, but offer her forgiveness, hope, and encouragement. Let her know the future can still be wonderful.

Everything that happens to us shapes us. Your daughter will never be the same, having gone through this experience (neither will you). Even though you would never have chosen this for her, you now have the opportunity to help her mature through this ordeal.

One of the most important things you can do is to allow your daughter to assume responsibility. She is facing some very difficult decisions. And she must live with the consequences of her decisions, so they must be hers. I am convinced that she will be wiser, stronger and better able to go on with life if she has shouldered her load in this process.

A young girl, much like your daughter, wrote these words several months after she had given birth to a baby and placed it for adoption:

"Perhaps all the heartbreak and painful memories have had some kind of purpose. It is so easy to forget what life is all about. What I have been through is a high price to pay for gaining maturity and faith in myself. I would never have chosen this experience, but in terms of my whole future, I would like to think it has been worthwhile."

I hope someday your daughter will feel good about herself, too. She needs all the support and understanding you are able to give. Right now, more than anything else, she needs *you*.

Lovingly,

Martha Zimmerman